YES, IT'S YOU

Self-Love Starts with Accountability

Written by Ann Akinnuoye

Title: Yes, It's You
By: Ann Akinnuoye
Edited by: 846 Publishing and Jessica Schmidt
Cover Design: 846Publishing.com

Copyright 2024
I S B N – 979-8-9904707-0-5
I S B N – 979-8-9904707-1-2
I S B N – 979-8-9904707-2-9

Library of Congress Control Number: 2024916351

DEDICATION

I dedicate this book to my two little sisters, Tolu and Tobi. Thank you for allowing me to be your big sister. Thank you for reminding me that our trials and triumphs need to be shared. Thank you for reminding me that God blesses us so we can bless other people.

Through our stories and experiences, we are all connected.

YES, IT'S YOU

TABLE OF CONTENTS

PROLOGUE

There was a time when any discussion of mental health was taboo. People lost jobs, sacrificed relationships, and suffered irreparable damage to their reputations for simply admitting they needed help. Similarly, conversations about self-awareness and self-love were not always welcomed. The good news is those days are gone.

I am extremely grateful for where we are as a society. It's amazing to see people embrace who they are while becoming aware of their own needs. Although we have made strides, we often miss a piece of the "self-love" puzzle. We focus so much on loving ourselves that we oftentimes forget that "loving ourselves" requires being honest with ourself as well. Honesty is necessary to do the real work. Honesty is a prerequisite to healing. That said, honesty isn't always fun. It doesn't look good. And it definitely doesn't feel good. Why, you ask? Honesty is acknowledging that the majority of our emotional and psychological wounds are self-inflicted. Honesty forces us to admit we may not like who we see in the mirror. It makes us address the damaging things we've done to others; and even sometimes to ourselves. There is no self-love without honesty. And there is no honesty without accountability.

I have to admit, writing this book has been one long therapy session for me. It made me question various parts of my own life. It provided an opportunity to discuss sensitive but necessary topics, while I engaged in conversations with people from all walks of life. I found myself dissecting why people (including me) say and do the things we do. I also explored why we behave the way we do.

My superpower has always been how direct I am. But sometimes it has also been my kryptonite. To be fair, I tend to be brutally honest. At times, the message gets lost in the delivery. I am painfully aware of this and have fought hard to find the balance between saying what needs to be said, while also making sure my style of delivery didn't stop the message from being received. I have internal struggles between who I am naturally and who I think I need to be in order to have genuine, long-standing friendships, and relationships. For a long time, I tried to bite my tongue when asked certain things. Or I would remain in situations to appease others to avoid uncomfortable moments for everyone involved. This led to two realizations. First, the problem was not my brutal honesty. It was partly my delivery (at times), and partly my desire to appease everyone. Second, as I looked more closely, I realized, my honesty forced people to face a multitude of truths they may not have been ready to face.

Oftentimes, we find ourselves in situations or dealing with emotions we do not like or even understand. Normally, it's due to choices we made in the past. When we do not take accountability for our thoughts, words, and actions, we end up moving through life being reactionary and leading with our ego or playing the victim.

If we sit and think for a moment, we all have a friend who can be a little abrasive. We love them. But they might not be the person we go to when we're looking for someone to tell us everything is okay; especially when it's not. We value their advice or perspective. Even though, we may not always want it. I tend to be that friend. Primarily, because I want people to hold me accountable for things I've done and said. So, I pride myself on holding those around me accountable, even when they don't ask; especially when they don't ask. I do this because I truly believe honesty that is not driven by emotion or even bias can be extremely insightful. Many of us go through life without self-reflection, and when you don't take the time to know who you are, while also being coddled, it can be a recipe for disaster and ingenuine relationships. Unfortunately, being that friend who is known to be a "truth-teller" doesn't always work out in my favor, but relationships built on this type of transparency are needed.

We must love people enough to be honest with them. Adult relationships thrive on honesty which demands accountability. There is no way for people to maintain genuine friendships without it. Now, if the desire is to cultivate surface level friendships, then feel free to ignore everything I just said. But, since you're reading this book, it's safe to say you desire deeper relationships, with yourself and others. Keep in mind, honesty and accountability can come with consequences. If you're willing to accept that, you'll be okay. You may not be the most popular, but the right people will gravitate towards you. The right people will value you. The right people will love you. Your tribe will find you. I learned that from experience. I had to do the work on myself through trial and error. I had to come to terms with the fact that sometimes my truth or opinion did not matter to other people, and I had to be okay with that.

Although I am a creative person at heart, I tend to have a very black-and-white viewpoint; at least when it comes to my core values and opinions. Sure, gray areas exist in our lives. But, we cannot constantly live there. We cannot exist in a world where we are constantly wavering between ideals. There must come a point when we decide who we are, what we believe, and what we stand for, good or bad. Life becomes easier when you deal with people and circumstances as they are; not as you wish them to be.

It's time to start asking yourself questions that will undoubtedly change your life for the better. Maybe not immediately, but definitely in the long run. This is a moment of introspection for those of us who have been too busy allowing life to happen to us. This is a reality check for those of us who are already on our self-love journey, but still need to do the real work.

This is the moment to acknowledge our lives are our responsibility.

Ann Akinnuoye

Chapter 1: Reality Check

We all have experienced moments of anger, sadness, doubt, and sometimes even depression. Most of us have moments in our past when we wish we had behaved differently. Or in some instances we wish we'd done nothing at all. Although it's impossible to change the past, we can use it to gain insight and improve how we react in the future. It's time for a reality check.

It is time to start asking ourselves the tough questions. Reflect on why you've made certain decisions and handled things in your life the way you have. Life may not always be sunshine and roses, but the hurt, and pain, can serve a purpose. These moments can serve as indicators to alert us when something is not right. These moments can also become catalysts for change and help us to make better decisions.

Without these moments of reflection, it would be difficult to make the necessary adjustments required to regain control over our lives. Without the hardships, some of us would never chase our goals with the utter persistence and resilience needed to accomplish them. Feeling unfulfilled can push us. Being unhappy can serve as ammo. We have moments in our lives when things may seem unbearable. It may also appear that everything is falling apart. These moments force us to take inventory of our lives and the decisions we've made. These moments allow us the space to have needed conversations with one another and oftentimes with ourselves. The exchanges may not be pretty. But, they are definitely necessary.

Through dealing with my own depression and ups and downs, I recognized I was running on autopilot. I was literally doing what I thought I should be doing. I did what was expected of me. I did what was necessary to pay the bills and stay afloat. I created this image that everything was fine on the outside. Meanwhile, I was slowly dying on the inside. I began to hate those around me, including myself. Then, something shifted. I realized not everyone was miserable. I knew people who were truly happy. They were kind, patient, courageous, and generous with their time and resources. They had real joy, and their energy was infectious. Most importantly, they had a level of calmness and peace I had never experienced. This shift made me realize I did not need to suffer. From the outside looking in, there was nothing dramatically different between me and them, besides the fact they seemed to be enjoying life regardless of what was going on around them. They seemed happy and confident.

See, I did not come from a home where happiness or confidence was necessarily instilled. I was just expected to be good, actually great. There was no real discussion about how or why I had to get straight As, be at the top of my class, work multiple jobs without complaint, or be the model student, employee, and daughter that stayed out of trouble. There was no room for mistakes. I was just expected to always be the best. An imaginary bar was set that I was expected to reach. The pressure of these expectations led to me seeing myself as a failure. Things got bad. There were times when I would not get out of bed for days or months at a time because it felt better to deal with things in isolation. Although, I wasn't really dealing with anything at all. I began comparing myself to the happy and successful people around me. I literally started stalking some of them online.

On the surface, they all seemed to have this positive attitude that "anything is possible, the world is my oyster." I knew whatever they were doing was working, at least better than what I was doing, which was not much. Change often happens only after we realize that something is wrong or "off" in our lives. This change only happens after you realize the need for a drastic pivot. Truly pivoting means assessing everything and everyone around you and holding yourself accountable for where you are in life and the decisions that have led you there.

I am sure if we all had it our own way, there would be no instances when we felt doubt, hatred, depression, etc. All of life's moments would be filled with nothing but bliss and positivity. Unfortunately, we do not live in a perfect world. We live in a world where there is duality. A world where there is good and bad. The only constant is change. The truth is, you cannot change your life until you decide to fully be present. You have to decide to deal with facts.

The funny thing about life is the worst of times may also be the inspiration and motivation to start on a path to turn your life completely around. When you change your perspective, you can see more clearly. We can acknowledge the toughest days equipped us for our best days. We are then able to look back, remember how far we've come, appreciate where we are, and envision our future possibilities.

Chapter 2: Know Your Why

Do you ever wonder why certain things are happening to you? Does it seem like you are going through the same scenarios over-and-over with different people? Does it feel like you are repeating behaviors that eventually lead to learning lessons you thought you've already mastered? It's time to start acknowledging and addressing repeated behaviors once and for all. This can be difficult because it is easier to point the finger at others rather than accepting the fact that "it is you." Nine out of ten times, you are the cause of your struggle, pain, and heartbreak. As sobering as that may be, you are not alone. Everyone who wants to improve their relationships with themselves and others has struggled with taking accountability at one point or another.

Every action has a reaction, cause, and effect. For the most part, outside of major trauma or tragic life-altering events, everything that has happened to you, good or bad, can be traced to a previous action, decision, or thought that was at least somewhat within your control. This might seem harsh, but it's a fact you need to face if you intend on doing better, or at least making different decisions in the future. When you get used to pointing the finger at other people, it becomes a habit to blame them for the way you act and the things you do. But when does it stop? When do you start to realize you need to look at the common denominator in each situation? In the times of darkness, the one constant is you.

When did you begin to notice the patterns? When did you start to realize you are in control of your reactions and behavior? It's not about anyone else or what they do. It is about you taking responsibility. When did you finally look in the mirror and begin to own your thoughts, words, actions, and circumstances? What if you were able to take complete control and responsibility for everything that happens to you? What if you welcomed the fact you have more control than you realize, or than you ever thought was possible? Now is the time to do the difficult and uncomfortable work of holding yourself accountable. Now that you have admitted you are the one holding yourself back, you can accept you are also the one who can set yourself free.

Once you realize this key fact, you truly start living. When you are no longer bound to the idea other people control your emotions, thoughts, actions, and destiny, that is when you start your self-love journey.

That is how you truly discover who you really are. Your purpose and what you want out of life become clear. This is when you create your own set of rules to live life by.

For a long time, I didn't know what my purpose was. I just knew I wanted to make my father proud. This thought and obligation stayed with me even after he passed. I knew I needed to be financially stable and completely independent. I just didn't know how to get there. From a young age, I saw what it was like to be loved, taken care of, and adored. I lived without a care in the world. Then, when he passed, I suddenly experienced what it felt like to be alone. I watched my mother struggle and work multiple jobs to make sure I was taken care of. Looking back on the pain I felt, I promised to do everything in my power to spare my future children the same fate. I never wanted my own children to see me working for people I disliked. I never wanted them to hear me complain about having to do a job I hated. I never wanted to depend on a man for anything.

In the past, before I started on my own self-knowledge journey, as life hit me with curveball after curveball, I decided I needed a break. The easiest way to take a break was to let life take its course. I no longer wanted to be an active participant in my life. After graduating from high school, I had a "plan" which was basically to follow the path to the "American dream." Unfortunately, I forgot the "American Dream" was not created with me in mind.

My plan was simple: go to a good school and graduate with a dual degree in accounting/finance, work at one of the big four firms, sit for my CPA, get married, and have kids. Although I graduated and even worked in private banking for a couple of years, it was during my junior year in college when I realized the rest of the plan would have to change.

I came to terms with the fact that being an accountant and sitting at a desk for eight hours or more each day was not for me. More than that, it would be a disservice to myself and potential clients to work in a field I was not passionate about. I never wanted the responsibility of ruining someone else's finances due to my lack of interest in a job. Now that I think about it, I was more concerned with destroying someone else's finances than I was about ruining my own life by continuing down a path of unfulfillment.

At the time, I didn't know what God put me on this earth to do. I only knew he had bigger plans for me. It was always there in my spirit. I always felt there was more, although I always fought against it. But, after a while, I grew tired of fighting. This exhaustion didn't result in a grand change. Instead, it led to a deep depression. I continued to watch life pass me by. I had no ambition or desire to change until the death of my cousin. He passed away in a car accident, days after his wife gave birth to their first son. I remember getting that call. I left my desk and never went back.

Chapter 3: Who Are You?

When people ask, "Who are you?" What is your initial response? Do you share your first name or last? Do you offer information about your children? Do you talk about your job description or title? Do you list your accomplishments?

It's a tough question. What defines you? What do you want to be known for? The way you answer this question says a lot about how you perceive yourself. It also shows how you want others to perceive you.

What are you most proud of? What is your biggest accomplishment to date? What do you see when you look in the mirror? Who is staring back at you? Are you proud of that person? Who are you in the world? Who are you when you are alone? Most people equate their value with their place in society. They allow cultural standards to dictate if they are successful or not. They compare their lives to the lives of others.

They are defined by other people's expectations, not their own. We aren't taught to stand out, or to create impactful change and go against the grain. Most of us are taught to follow the rules that were set by our parents, our teachers, our bosses, our peers, and sometimes our romantic partners. We want to fit in with the masses. We want to be accepted. And we want to be liked, even if that means never finding out who we are. Or worse, losing ourselves as individuals to become who someone else wants us to be. We have been taught our wants and needs should align with the masses. But should they?

How many times have you stopped yourself from doing or saying something because you feared how others would perceive you or react? How many times have you second-guessed your life decisions because they were not what others expected of you? How many times have you allowed the opinions of others to stop you from living your own truth? Every time you make a decision based on the thoughts of others; you start to lose yourself bit by bit without even realizing it. You unconsciously fall in love with things that make you unhappy. And, by the time you realize what is happening, one-third, one-half, or three-fourths of your life has been wasted.

We would like to think we are living our lives for ourselves. But, in fact, most of us are subconsciously living for everyone else. We do things simply to make others happy or "keep the peace." But are you really keeping the peace if everyone is at peace besides you?

People mean well, but, what if your good intentions were still detrimental to yourself and those you love? Being thoughtful of others is a noble thing. That said, you must always consider your motives. Are you giving to others from a place of joy and abundance? Or, are you giving out of fear and lack?

When you give too much of yourself, eventually you will be left with nothing. If you always give to others without taking time to care for yourself, there will come a point when you have nothing else to give. And, when you are completely depleted, not only will you resent those closest to you, but they will also come to resent you. Why? Because people who were accustomed to constantly taking from you will no longer value or need you once you have nothing left to offer.

There is absolutely nothing wrong with doing for others. It is honorable and we should all strive to do so. At the same time, it is important to remember the best way to help people in the long run is to do so from a healthy place. That requires knowing who you are, setting appropriate boundaries, and taking care of yourself. Self-care and self-love are extremely important to our overall well-being and play a key role in how much you can genuinely give to other people. Doing acts of kindness with a hateful, or envious heart will always leave you empty. There is a correlation between how happy and healthy you are and how well you treat the people around you. Happy people operate from a different space. Happy people can be kind to others without feeling drained or used. Happy people maneuver through life differently!

When you get to know yourself, you start to understand your wants, needs, flaws, motivations, quirks, non-negotiables, and obsessions. Understanding who you are is one of the most important and profound things you can do as an adult. You can keep everyone at arm's length, except yourself. You cannot hide from yourself. You can try, but sooner or later it becomes cancerous to your overall well-being. With other people, you may be guarded. You may go days, months, and years pretending things are okay. You may talk about everything except the things that truly matter, but that is impossible to do long-term without serious repercussions and damage to yourself. Sooner or later, you will feel the effects of being deceptive by lying and pretending. You may crave a safe place to let it all out. You may start questioning whether the relationships you've built are genuine because you are surrounded by people you cannot be yourself around. This may lead to self-hatred. You will indirectly begin mistreating yourself simply because you didn't take the time to figure out who you are.

Not knowing who you are, or failing to come to grips with who you are, can make you susceptible to depression and anxiety. It can lead to a variety of problems that will only worsen over time. It may be the reason you continue to find yourself in different predicaments. You are the only person who knows your deep dark secrets. You know what you've been through, what has brought you to your knees in desperation, and what you've overcome. You are the only person who has the key to the Pandora's box that is your life. You must be willing to open the box without fear. Otherwise, you will always be held hostage by the secrets inside. The longer you continue to hide from yourself, the longer it will take to have true freedom and eventually peace.

You may be your own biggest roadblock and your own worst nightmare. Do not allow your thoughts, actions, or the fear of other people's opinions to hinder or emotionally impede you from growing. Getting to know yourself will be an experience like no other. It is a never-ending journey. There is no written test. But life will administer a series of lessons. Through these lessons, you will be forced to make decisions that will either create a better version of yourself, provide insight, or require you to come face-to-face with the fact that you may be your biggest hurdle. Lean in and don't fight the process.

You must be honest with yourself to truly learn these lessons. Sometimes, we lie to ourselves about what we truly want and need. We fear the truth. Never deprive yourself of something you want (within reason) simply because you think it's unattainable. You must be okay with not always receiving what you want, but to pretend it's not something you desire does more harm than good. Be honest with your emotions, actions, fears, and thoughts. When you do this, you are able to tap into something very special. You'll uncover the key to real transformation if you trust the process and allow it to happen for you.

Knowing who you are means acknowledging and addressing the changes you need to make to become the best version of yourself. You should always be willing to evolve. That is done by facing your flaws, mistakes, and insecurities. Before you can change habits, you must first identify them. Yes, we can be amazing people. However, we can also be mean, devious, manipulative, lazy, and bitter people. You must be okay with knowing who you are—the good, bad, and ugly. You must recognize and take responsibility for your shortcomings. Or, what I like to call your "quirks." Until you do that, you will never be able to change your present behavior and circumstances. The life you are living today is the result of the choices you made yesterday, last month, last year, etc. Where you will be a year from now depends on the choices you make today. Make decisions today your future self will be proud of.

How often do you self-evaluate? Most people are so afraid of facing who they really are that they run from it at all costs. They fear what they will discover. They fear not being able to live up to the same standards they set for other people; they fear being viewed as a hypocrite, or, even worse, a fraud.

They are scared they might discover they are not the great people they portray themselves to be. They fear judgment from others.

People fear the truth.

None of us is perfect. We are not meant to be. We are human and there is nothing wrong with that. Be who you are and set out to be the best version of yourself. Accepting your humanity is the first step.

Self-discovery is not about overanalyzing everything you've done, said, or thought. It's a process to identify or develop who you are when no one is looking. What brings you happiness? What are your fears? What are your triggers? It's about becoming comfortable with who you are when all the masks are removed.

People have forgotten how wonderful it is to just be ourselves. It is freeing. It is revolutionary. We get so caught up in our careers, relationships, friends, and even family that we lose sight of our wants and needs. We lose sight of what truly brings us joy. The goal in writing this book is to make it acceptable to have intimate conversations with oneself. It's an opportunity for each of us to embrace our flaws and come face-to-face with our insecurities. We all have imperfections and areas we can improve, but that should not stop us from embracing who we are at our core. As long as you accept responsibility for your thoughts, actions, and emotions, you are living in your truth. Apart from whatever higher power you believe in, you are the only person who has real control and power over your life. You have all the necessary tools, even if it does not feel like it.

Realizing how much authority you have over your life is liberating. It's life changing. When you no longer allow your flaws, fears, and mistakes to control you, they lose power. They simply become a part of your story. Taking ownership and regaining control does not mean things will always work out in your favor. It does mean you have the ability to alter how you perceive the things that happen in your life. When something no longer has a hold on you, it cannot be used as a weapon against you. Your past may never completely go away, but it can be utilized for something constructive and beautiful. There is power in honesty and accountability.

Be real. Be genuine. Be You!

During my own journey of self-knowledge and self-discovery, I had to come to terms with my past. This gave me the freedom to welcome thoughts of the future. When I sat down and really accepted who I was and who I wanted to be, I created a bold proclamation for myself. I hope sharing mine encourages you to explore who you truly are.

Who am I? I am a God-fearing woman who has learned to love life in all its phases. I am a Nigerian woman who can't wait to be a wife and mother and to share all the love I have within me. I am a woman who sometimes questions whether I will have time to raise a family or achieve the career goals I set for myself. I am a woman who lost her father at the age of nine and never stops thinking about how my life would be different if he were still alive. I am a person who hates the term "strong woman." I am a hopeless romantic who can be vicious when provoked. At times, I may treat the people I love harshly. I am someone who experiences real joy from seeing smiles on the faces of people I care for. I am a carefree little girl who still seeks the approval of my brothers because they remind me of my father. I am still that little girl who gets insecure at times, but knows she was wonderfully and beautifully made. I am resilient. I am a force to be reckoned with. I am a daughter who butts heads with her mother. Yet, I have come to realize every disagreement or argument was fueled by the love she has for me. I am a businesswoman and now an author who relishes creating, managing, and strategizing how to scale several businesses. I am a negotiation machine. I am a woman who has a soft spot for people who are brave enough to make their own way in life. I am stubborn and very private, to the point that my actions sometimes seem secretive. I am an overthinker. I am a sister, a daughter, and an aunt. I am a trauma survivor. I am all these things and more.

Chapter 4: Choosing Happiness

Perception is everything, it can sometimes be more powerful than reality. Many of us wear masks, play a role, and act as others expect. But are we truly happy? What is happiness? When do you know you are happy? When do you know you are not just content, but truly, undeniably happy? Do you believe you are allowed happiness? Is real happiness even a goal for people anymore? For some, happiness has turned into some mystical thought or aesthetic to be displayed on our social media feeds. While others may think happiness is a destination that can only be reached once they obtain some level of success, fame, or socioeconomic status.

Happiness has not always been a priority for a lot of us, not real happiness anyway. Sure, the happiness we thought came after achieving our goals was always part of the conversation, but happiness that is not tied to a place, thing, or person often gets put on the back burner. Life got in the way and people were more concerned with doing whatever it took to get by. We were not taught to chase what truly made us happy; we are taught to chase what makes us money, what makes us less likely to get hurt, or what makes us successful by societal standards. Happiness turned into something that felt complicated and remained elusive. We speak of happiness as if it is some lofty notion only a few have the privilege of experiencing.

Happiness is not a privilege; it is a choice. A consistent and intentional choice. It is a state of being. None of us were put on this earth to be miserable or live a life full of suffering. We have the right to be happy. A right we must protect. You must make a conscious decision to attain and maintain true happiness that is not constantly wavering. That decision must be made daily and requires a new level of honesty and accountability. Under normal circumstances our happiness is within our control. I say "normal" because we cannot ignore the reality that some people are completely unable to control their thoughts or actions. In those situations, a medical professional may need to intervene. I would be remiss in only acknowledging a one-size fits all scenario.

For the rest of us, true happiness starts with self. Nothing you do externally will bring you lasting happiness. No amount of money, sex, external praise, drugs, or success can bring you real happiness. Who are you, and how do you feel about yourself when you are stripped of all your masks? Are you happy? If the pandemic taught us one thing, it's that you cannot hide from yourself forever. Sooner or later, you will have to come face to face with YOU.

Regardless of what you have or who is in your life, if you are not happy, every aspect of your life will be affected. You will continue to mask your unhappiness until it eventually becomes a cancer. Unhappiness can and will eat you alive from the inside out. It can start with small comparisons, which can lead to a jaded or warped perspective, which can manifest into depression. You will become a slave to the very thing you want so desperately to escape. You will be consumed by everything you perceive as an obstacle. You will be so focused on putting on a facade for others, trying so hard not to be unhappy, but subconsciously that is exactly what you will become. Without realizing it, the negative self-talk, the chaos in and around you, the unresolved trauma, the difficult conversations you've avoided, the blame you put on others, the lack of honesty and self-reflection will begin to weigh on you, and if you are not careful it will cause a domino effect in all areas of your life. What you feed will grow.

The natural twists and turns of life make being happy all the time nearly impossible. Life will throw things your way that will make you cry, scream, fight, and want to hide. Life is never short of a plot twist. Your life can change in seconds. It may never be smooth sailing the entire ride. You will have your days, weeks, months, and even years of tumultuous times, and you will have your share of breaking points. These are the moments when having deep-rooted happiness and joy to rely on will be paramount.

Happiness is not a destination or a feeling that can be turned on and off. It's a never-ending journey. Our happiness can and will look different through the various phases of our lives. It may show up louder for some or radiate in moments of stillness for others. The key is to always have a reference for what happiness looks like, feels like, and means to you regardless of what's going on in the world. You must be unapologetically intentional about creating and maintaining happiness for yourself. You are not defined by what you've gone through, what you have lost, or your mistakes. Yes, those are all parts of your story, but not who you are, and definitely not a reason to give away your power, or your right to be happy.

At the core, happiness is knowing, accepting, and loving who you are. Being happy means acknowledging your flaws, owning your decisions, learning from every experience, and taking back control of your life. We only have one life to live, and yes, they say it's short, but it is also the longest experience you'll have while on earth. If you don't take back your power and actively decide to be happy or pursue happiness, one day you will wake up and realize you are living a life that was created for you, not by you. You cannot be passive about your happiness.

There is a purpose for all of it. One of the simplest ways to create or maintain a state of happiness is learning to be appreciative of everything, from the air we breathe to the stranger who held the elevator doors open. Appreciating the small things teaches our minds to gravitate towards gratitude and positivity instead of complaining or negativity. It trains our minds to seek and acknowledge the good, rather than harping on the bad.

Life will hit you with curve balls, but when you have done the work, are self-aware, practice radical honesty and self-love, and hold yourself accountable, it becomes easier to return to happiness, or at the very least gratitude. If your happiness is solely based on other people and things, you can never return to happiness because you never truly had it. You will continue to ride whatever wave your life currently has you on, constantly seeking out people and things to fill a void that only you are equipped to fill. When your happiness comes from within, you are not easily devastated or controlled by external circumstances. As the saying goes, you might bend, but you will not break.

You need to know the source of your happiness; you can't place that power in the hands of anyone else. What makes you genuinely happy? What would you put everything on the line for? Those are the things that deserve your time and energy. Those are the moments we should chase.

In a society where the idea of the "American Dream" has been shoved down everyone's throats, most of us have become so complacent because we have allowed society to dictate what our purpose and lives should look like. We have forgotten to ask ourselves, "How do I want to live?" How many of us have given up on our dreams before even really giving them a shot? How many of us just run on the hamster wheel of life, doing things for the sake of doing them without any real desire or understanding? We just want to do enough so we aren't labeled failures, condemned, or laughed at by our peers. We do not want to be judged by society.

The truth is, we can't do what makes us happy or fulfills us, because we have not taken the time to get to know ourselves well enough to pinpoint what that is. We are so busy chasing what we believe to be the "American Dream," we forgot about our own.

You must make a conscious choice to be happy. Your happiness begins and ends with you. Happiness is a state of being, it's not a temporary emotion. Happiness is acknowledging who you are, and even who you aren't, and being completely okay with that. At this moment, are you happy? Are you happy with the life you are living, with the life you have created?

Being a happy person is not always an easy choice. Many times, falling into negativity, self-pity, or finger pointing takes a lot less work, awareness, honesty, control, and discipline. If you are unhappy, you must figure out why and proactively make decisions that support a different version of yourself. The moment you forget the choice begins with you; is the moment you have handed over your power. Never allow other people and things to dictate what your happiness looks and feels like. True happiness requires accountability. It's important to note that taking accountability does not mean accepting fault or blame. It simply means you identified the role you played, big or small, accepted the situation and sought a solution, and now you are focused on moving forward. You have chosen to take your happiness into your own hands.

Things are not always as complicated as we make them. Find out what makes you happy, do it, and do it often. It's that simple. Stop overthinking. Enjoy the simplicity of life. Release the past and resist grieving over things that could have been. Life is meant to be lived and enjoyed. Are you enjoying your life? Or, are you complaining about how things could have been different? Are you counting your blessings? Or, are you comparing your life to someone else's? The consequences of choosing to live for others will be yours to bear. Until you let go of how you imagined things would be and come to terms with your current reality, you will never truly know happiness.

If I told you no one has ever cared about me, or I've always been alone, it would probably make these words more impactful, but it would also make me a liar. I may not have been alone, but I have felt alone, invisible, unworthy, belittled, and unloved. I remember when I was going through a really rough time, and people would ask, "How are you," I would look at them in the eye with a smile on my face and reply with one of my routine lies:

- ☐ "I'm good!"
- ☐ "I'm great."
- ☐ "I'm fine."
- ☐ "I'm blessed and highly favored."

I said whatever was necessary to end the conversation and keep the attention away from how I was actually feeling. I never wanted people to pity me, or know that I was broke, unhappy, or suffering on the inside. Instead, I needed them to believe the story I told. I needed them to believe I was good, so they would leave me alone. I was more concerned with looking happy and telling everyone I was happy, than I was with being happy. It wasn't until I recognized the same deceitful and hurtful actions in someone I cared about that I realized I was doing myself a disservice by pretending. I was wearing a mask.

I needed to talk to someone, I needed to refocus, I needed to work on myself. I needed to figure out why I was so miserable and why my emotions were all over the place. It literally felt like I was feeling everything and nothing, all at the same time. I was going through my days with a smile on my face while it felt like I was dying on the inside.

Looking back, I realize the pretending only prolonged my pain because pretending to be okay is draining. I never wanted to be a burden. I was so concerned with how I made other people feel that I forgot to take care of myself. I could not be of any real use to those I cared about until I took a hard look at my own life and began taking the necessary steps to make changes. I had to own all the things I thought, said, and did that contributed to where I was mentally and emotionally. I had to hold myself accountable.

Chapter 5: What about Boundaries

Society has subconsciously taught us to accept certain behaviors. To keep the peace, we stay in harmful or inappropriate relationships regardless of the consequences. We excuse disrespect and mistreatment. But, why? Some would say "hurt people hurt people" to justify said behavior. However, I would like to challenge that by asking you a question. Do a person's life experiences excuse their bad behavior? Or is it our duty to teach people how to treat us?

It's necessary to hold people accountable for the way they treat you. Unfortunately, people tend to explain away bad behavior or worse, refuse to acknowledge it is happening. It can be easier to turn a blind eye to avoid confrontation. You don't risk the discomfort of offense or change when you remain silent.

By constantly making excuses for someone and allowing behaviors to slide, you become an enabler. You fall into a pattern of rewarding actions that should be reprimanded. This creates a vicious cycle. Saying nothing, in turn, sets a precedent for future behavior. It communicates that bad behavior is not only accepted but welcomed. You inadvertently teach people to mistreat you. Believe it or not, some people are unaware of their actions because they were never held accountable. If no one brings it to their attention, how will they learn to self-correct the issue? You must tell people how their words or actions made you feel. Letting people do you harm without any fear of consequences is equivalent to a get-out-of-jail-free card. Bad behavior that is not corrected will be repeated.

Life is interesting. You will notice you often get treated the worst by people who mean the most to you. It's not because they don't love you. It's simply because you allow it. You may fear them becoming angry, leaving, or losing whatever position you had in their life if you speak up. This is evident in friendships, romantic interactions, and business relationships. When you fear things ending, you are reluctant to rock the boat in any capacity. So, you endure pain, disrespect, and neglect with the hope of keeping this person in your life; even if their presence does more harm than good.

Establishing clear boundaries and practicing self-care means having the courage to realize you deserve better and then learn how to demand it from others. Let's be clear, most of you deserve better friendships, relationships, and business partnerships. You deserve a life full of love, appreciation, and respect. You deserve to be around people who do not make you question your worth. You deserve happiness. Holding people accountable may be difficult at first, but it will strengthen the right relationships. When you speak up, you are advocating for yourself and what you deserve.

You cannot expect everyone to have the same moral compass. Let people know when and how they have hurt you. People who truly love you will appreciate your honesty, while others may lash out or withdraw. Don't be afraid to stand your ground or simply let them go. Be okay with letting go of things and people that do not fit into the life you choose for yourself. Everyone has different expectations, upbringings, and triggers. Until you tell people what your boundaries are, you cannot expect them to know how to interact with you. You must teach people how to interact with you; especially those you love. Communication is vital to any successful relationship. Do not be afraid to address any issues or concerns that arise. Remember, once you have allowed a pattern to develop, it may take a few reminders to help people adjust to your new requirements and boundaries. For those that refuse to change, you must be willing to hold yourself and them accountable. This may also result in removing people from your life.

Your life is a reflection of your decisions. When you become a proactive participant in your relationships and not just reactive, life will become dramatically less complicated. If you continue to be passive and approach things timidly, your life will become a reflection of that as well. You have the power. You have the control. If you feel powerless or disrespected, ask yourself, "Why am I allowing this person to treat me this way?" Take a moment to assess. Then, take back your power by correcting their bad behavior immediately. This is essential to preserve your mental health.

It's important not to allow people to get too comfortable if their comfort means you are disregarded. There must be balance, which can be created by introducing healthy boundaries. Boundaries can be difficult to set; especially when your nature is to be open. But being open too soon with the wrong people can be life altering. When you overshare information about yourself, people mistake that as a license to dig further. You are not obligated to divulge more than you are comfortable with sharing. Boundaries help create an environment where healthy relationships can grow.

Take a moment and ask yourself, do you feel you are constantly being disrespected? Are people always belittling you or making you feel inadequate? If so, then you must reevaluate your relationships. It is one thing to set boundaries. But it is another to stick to them and make sure no one crosses them. Once a person crosses your boundaries without any consequences, they will continue to ignore them. It is human nature to test limitations. People like to see what they can get away with.

You have to be careful when and how you give others access to you. When you share too much too soon, people may not value you as they should. That's why boundaries are necessary. People need to know what lines not to cross. Remember, if you do not set limits for people, they will set them for you. Boundaries protect you by creating guardrails around your most prized possession…YOU!

It can be easy to blame your friends and family for the way they treated you. We have all had our share of victim moments. From the outside looking in, it could be said I have a hard exterior. The reality is, I am sensitive and can be a pushover when it comes to the people I love. Because of this, my time, money, and energy were often taken advantage of. I would find myself in positions where my desire to be loved and valued left me depleted. I knew my family and friends did not intend to maliciously hurt me, but that didn't make the betrayal any less painful. Years ago, I ended up over $50,000 in debt because I decided to assist someone very close to me. I was heartbroken. More importantly, I was disappointed that people I loved and respected took advantage of me in a major way. I failed to stand up for myself. I had no boundaries in place.

Life got dark. I started to question my worth and existence due to the situations I continuously found myself in. Things had to change. I realized people did things to me they thought they could get away with. At that moment, I had to question the relationship I had with myself. That empowered me to evaluate how I allowed others to treat me as well. It was hard putting boundaries up with people; especially when all I wanted was to love and help others.

I had a constant internal struggle between who I was, who I wanted to be, and who I needed to be. I can't say I was never hurt or taken advantage of again, but I was able to better discern between those who loved me and those who were using me. I began to speak up in instances when I would have previously let things slide. I had to set boundaries to maintain my peace and happiness. This was not the easiest thing to do, but it was necessary. As a result, some relationships had to be severed.

One of those relationships was an ex-friend and business partner—someone I considered family. Over the years our connection changed. Things were good between us, until they weren't. The mutual respect we once had was no longer there. It began with verbal jabs in private followed by public disrespect. At first, I laughed it off, but, as the attacks became more vicious and personal, I could no longer ignore what was going on. I had to take the blinders off and understand the reason they continued to treat me the way they did was because I allowed it. As time went on, I could no longer tolerate their behavior! I had to create boundaries. Initially, these new boundaries strained our relationship. We didn't speak for months. We were distant.

Although it hurt and I felt uncomfortable with our new dynamic, the boundaries were necessary. It took some time, but after a while, we were able to have a constructive and respectful conversation. This led to mutual understanding. Did things go back to how they once were? No. But I was ok with that, because the dynamic of our relationship needed to change in order to maintain my self-respect. It showed the other person I deserved to be treated with care and common decency. More importantly, it revealed I was willing to distance myself if they continued to treat me poorly. As a result, the mutual respect we once had slowly returned. Boundaries are not always about keeping people out. They equally help determine who values, respects, and wants you in their life.

Chapter 6: Love Is Not Enough

Love is beautiful. It can creep into your heart without notice or warning. Love does not come with a set of guidelines, and it often rejects boundaries. Love is free-flowing. Most people crave love and intimacy. The problem with love is everyone's experience is different. What is love? Can you have a successful relationship based on love alone? Many people would answer yes. Others may agree love is one of the most amazing experiences a person can have, but then argue you cannot sustain a long-term relationship on love alone.

We all have our own definitions of love. If you ask one person, they may define love as a relationship built on respect and fidelity. While another may define love as compassion and empathy. If two people claim they love each other but define love differently, sooner or later, someone is going to feel like they are missing out. Clichй question, what is your love language? Is it the same in every relationship? How do your parents give and receive love? What about your siblings, friends, romantic partner, or your child? Have you asked or do you just assume?

Part of taking accountability for your life means taking responsibility for your heart. This includes knowing how you give and receive love. Once you identify your love language, it is vital you effectively communicate it to those you cherish while being mindful it may differ from person to person. For instance, if you need "words of affirmation" but your partner expresses love by buying you a gift, you may always feel unfulfilled. As a result, frustration arises. Neither of you are wrong. However, these differences should be communicated. Otherwise, it could lead to major complications in your relationship.

You can tell a person you love them day-in and day-out. You can write letters professing your love, sing songs, send tweets, or post each other's photos on Instagram. You can do all these things, and still fail to make them feel loved. People want to feel heard and seen. You do this by making an effort to communicate that through their love language. Understanding how a person gives and receives love shows effort and consideration. If your child, brother, friend, or partner expects love in a manner you are unable to give, there will always be an emotional game of tug-of-war at play. Think about the people closest to you and how they show you love in different ways; can you imagine how these differences can cause confusion and problems in interpersonal relationships? Let's break it down further.

If two people give and receive love differently, their love may never be fully understood or appreciated. Love and communication go hand in hand. In any relationship, whether platonic or intimate, it is important to express to your partner how you are feeling. If your love language is vastly different from theirs, continuing the relationship may become harder than it needs to be and end up being more trouble than it's worth. The reality is just because you love a person doesn't mean you should be together. Relationships require honesty, patience, understanding, accountability, and the willingness to compromise. I'd like to believe love, in some capacity, is part of every healthy relationship. I realize it's important. But I also recognize it's not the only factor.

To sustain a healthy, long-term relationship, your love for one another cannot be based on feelings alone. Genuine love is more than just an emotion. Feelings change all the time. True love is an action, a commitment, a conscious and active choice. Love is a decision. Never tell a person you love them unless you are willing to accept the responsibility that comes with that decision. You cannot truly love someone with one foot in and one foot out. Love cannot be based on emotions alone, because emotions come and go. Real love is never-ending, always evolving, and forever growing.

Many relationships end due to a lack of communication and compromise. If two people are unwilling to express their love the way the other needs to receive it, that love may fall on deaf ears and an unresponsive heart. This is not to say people with different love languages cannot have healthy relationships. It's just important to note it will require vulnerability, honesty, transparency, and patience from both parties. On the flip side, not all love is meant to be romantic. You can love a person without the need to be in a romantic relationship. Everyone needs and deserves love, but you may not be compatible with everyone you love.

Love is amazing. Love is beautiful when it is nurtured and reciprocated. It can make you feel safe and seen. Love heals and transforms, but it also comes with responsibility. If you are not careful or do not take the commitment that comes with it seriously, it can be as disastrous as it is beautiful. It can scar you so deeply it erodes you from the inside. There is power in love. It can be used to build people up and it can also be used to destroy.

The word love is often weaponized. To have something that is meant to be freeing used as a weapon can cause you to question everything you thought was true. It may make you fearful of intimacy and vulnerability. All love is not created equal and all that is labeled as love is not healthy. It can be controlling, self-serving, and used to manipulate. You can love wrong and be loved wrong. When you are mistreated under the falsehood of love, the aftermath from the experience can be devastating.

Receiving the wrong kind of love can cause depression, low self-esteem, mental, emotional, and even physical pain. It can lead to a distrust of others, or manifest in the form of self-sabotage. When you tell someone you love them, you are also telling them they can trust you with their whole being. You are saying you are willing and able to show up for them. And, often, this is where many are unable to deliver. Love is a decision; it means being responsible and accountable for how you treat people you claim to love. If you sit back and evaluate your past relationships, I guarantee the deepest hurt and betrayal came from those you loved or those who claimed to love you.

When you open your heart to others, you are allowing yourself to be vulnerable which can lead to possibly being hurt in the process, that's life. There is nothing you can do about it. What you can control is your reaction and how you respond to the actions of others. Don't hold on to the pain of failed relationships or the hurt they may have caused.

Use it. Learn from it. Grow from it.

Chapter 7: Feelings Are Not Facts

Humans are emotional creatures. That said, you should not be led by your emotions. Your emotions are your responsibility—no one else's. How many times have you put the responsibility for how you feel in the hands of others? How often have your emotions clouded your judgment? Have you ever focused solely on your feelings while ignoring all the facts? People often say, "Go with your heart" when it comes to making decisions. Yes, you should follow your heart. But never forget to bring your brain along for the ride.

Your emotions tend to lead you towards decisions that feel good in the moment. They fuel our desire for instant gratification. Whereas your mind can provide various perspectives and weigh in on the long-term pros and cons. Relying solely on either one to make a decision can be risky. You've heard it before, "Never make permanent decisions based on temporary emotions." If you act only on emotion, your plans will constantly change by the week, the day, the hour, or the minute. This can be a recipe for chaos.

When you solely depend on your feelings to make sense of situations where your objective, logic, and critical thinking skills may be of better use, things can often end up worse than how they started.

Acting on emotion is like feeding a monster. When you feed the monster, you strengthen the monster. Whatever you feed will grow. Sometimes feeding your emotions can lead to feeding your ego, which rarely ends well. While I would not recommend solely relying on your emotions, it is healthy to explore your emotions within reason. They do serve a purpose. Just be careful not to give in to them too freely. Otherwise, they could control every aspect of your life. Emotions are powerful. But, so are you.

How often have you blamed your emotions for your actions? Some may argue that emotions can make you do things you normally wouldn't have done. I disagree. Emotions don't make you do anything. People tend to use emotions as a scapegoat instead of holding themselves accountable. Being accountable allows you to take control of your emotions and your life. As complicated as they may be, the best way to deal with emotions is to create a safe space to acknowledge and feel them. That does not mean everything, or everyone deserves an emotional response. That's why it is important to create an emotional budget.

An emotional budget will create space to have better control over our fluctuating feelings, it puts us back in control. When you are not constantly being swayed by your emotions, you are able to make intentional decisions that have been properly thought through. It is important to know how to compartmentalize different situations, relationships, or experiences and react accordingly.

When creating an emotional budget, you must take inventory of every aspect of your life from personal relationships to finances. You take stock of how you react when things go right and wrong. An emotional budget does not mean you turn your emotions off. Instead, you evaluate what requires an emotional response, which allows you to focus on people and things that are important and stops you from exerting energy on areas better left alone. There is a time and place for everything, which can be easily forgotten when you are too caught up in your ever-changing emotions.

Not everyone should have unlimited access to your love, attention, and emotions. However, if you're anything like me, you want to give freely of yourself to those you care about. You want to help others as much as you can. Although this is noble, when is enough... well, enough? This was something I struggled with constantly.

In the past, I was always a shield for a particular friend. I was the person she would come to when there was a conflict with her significant other. If a crisis arose in her career, I was the person she would ask for advice. Or if she had a bad day, I was the friend she would come running to and share every issue with. At first, it was great. I enjoyed being her shoulder to cry on. As the years went on, I realized the relationship was terribly one-sided. The bottom line was I could not count on her like she counted on me. She was not emotionally available during my times of need. There was zero reciprocity.

As time passes, you realize you cannot continue to give from an empty cup. I had to make a conscious decision to ensure I filled my cup before giving to others. To successfully do this, I had to take a hard look at all my relationships. I had to make sure I was okay before concerning myself with others. Initially, it was not easy. The boundaries I set allowed me to see the friendship for what it was versus what I wanted it to be. No longer being clouded by emotion made it possible to acknowledge what we needed from one another and allowed us to define what a healthy relationship looked like in comparison to the history of our friendship. At the core, it could no longer be one person giving while the other person solely took. There had to be reciprocity.

We were able to rectify our differences. If I allowed my emotions to lead me, I would have continued to suffer in silence or lash out. Not to mention, our friendship would have remained strained. You see, emotions are tricky. You must make a conscious effort to acknowledge and address them, without allowing them to dictate your every move. You have to stay in control of your emotions.

53

Chapter 8: The Gift of Solitude

Check in with yourself. When was the last time you intentionally spent time alone without the distraction of music, a book, or another vice? We get so busy in the routine of life we forget to check in with ourselves. You must create space for yourself. Alone time is a necessity. It allows you to create space for reflection and introspection. Solitude provides the opportunity to genuinely figure out what matters most and provides an opportunity to sit with your thoughts, emotions, and perspectives without interruption.

You cannot truly enjoy and accept people for who they are until you learn to enjoy and accept who you are. This requires creating alone time for yourself. This means being comfortable in silence. When you are, you start to realize how much of your daily life is filled with noise. Sometimes the noise is people, social media, useless conversations, online shopping, partying, watching tv/streaming, or other forms of distractions. Alone time is essential because it forces you to get to know the person you spend the most time with, yourself.

Discover who you are. What are your likes and dislikes? Have conversations with yourself. Create goals and hobbies that are yours alone. Don't become so consumed with other people you forget who you are as an individual. The moment you lose yourself because you are trying to appease those around you is the moment you are no longer in control of your life. This results in unhealthy codependency. When your happiness is dependent on someone else it transfers the power out of your hands and into the hands of others. This can be harmful and limiting. It's okay to want the company of others but be sure to also enjoy the joy and sacredness of your own company. You cannot hide from yourself.

There is a difference between being alone and being lonely. Being alone is a result of not having anyone within your immediate proximity. While feeling loneliness could occur while in a room full of people. One deals with a physical occurrence while the other addresses an emotional/psychological state of mind.

Of course, we all want someone to share our lives with. We want to be around people who are in tune with our wants and needs. We need people who understand our personality and still decide to love us despite our flaws. We want people that feel like home. There is a familiar saying, "home is where the heart is." I always refer to this whenever people ask me if I miss home or if I am lonely due to traveling so much. But honestly, you can make "home" anywhere. If home is where the heart is, then I would argue I am always at home. Being alone can be the gift we didn't know we needed. It can be the gateway to self-discovery. When you lean in and embrace solitude you create space to find out who you truly are. You give yourself permission to explore what you truly need, i.e., honesty, love, grace, understanding, and clarity. There is power in being alone.

I encourage you to start having tough conversations with yourself. Challenge yourself to have the type of conversation that will force you to make noticeable changes in your life. This can only happen through accountability. When you know who you are as a person and create a safe place for yourself, independent of outside forces, loneliness does not exist. Once you realize being alone does not mean being lonely, your perspective changes. Life takes on a whole new meaning. You will revel in your newfound appreciation for "me" time.

Sooner or later, everyone will be forced to be alone in some capacity. It's better to approach those moments with a spirit of gratitude instead of fear. It might be for a day, a week, a month, or years, whether it's being single, being an only child, or happenstance. At some point, being alone is inevitable, but the feeling of loneliness is a choice. Although it can be uncomfortable, in the long run you will never regret learning about and spending time by yourself. You may even find you enjoy alone time the most.

There were moments when I was in a room filled with family and friends, but I still felt alone. This was loneliness. People told me they loved me. Yet, I didn't feel it. Instead, I felt misunderstood, judged, and even invisible. There was nothing anyone could say to make me feel better. I was dealing with something I could not explain. I was embarrassed by these emotions, and I thought no one would understand. It wasn't until I stopped running away from these feelings that I began to understand they served a purpose. I learned so much about myself during those moments of solitude. When you feel alone, you are forced to go back to the basics. You have to figure out what truly makes you happy. When you stop pretending, you can heal. You gain an awareness that forces you to find yourself or sometimes reinvent yourself.

In order to rebuild who you are, you must admit you are broken.

Chapter 9: The Blessing in Failed Relationships

I have this theory on relationships. The relationship that causes the most heartache and pain is not usually with the person you are meant to be with in the long run. However, they do still serve a purpose. Crossing paths with one another can and most likely will result in something even more beautiful. I find that these failed partnerships teach us the most about ourselves, including what we really want from others. They force us to hold ourselves and others accountable. Regardless of whether the relationship is platonic or romantic.

In a romantic relationship, the person who hurts you the most is unlikely to be part of your happily ever after. The person who caused you the most misery is not expected to be your "soul mate" or your "forever." To have a long-lasting, meaningful, healthy relationship (key word: healthy), there must be some boundaries that are never crossed. There must be a certain level of respect that is always upheld by both parties. We are human, and each have our own set of values, triggers, insecurities, and limits. What might be a non-issue for you, can be the cause of pain for someone else. There are things that, once they transpire, will forever change the dynamic of the relationship.

Look at it this way, the person who causes you intense pain will break you down emotionally and spiritually. They will take you to a place that is nearly impossible to come back from. You will be emotionally scarred and when the relationship ends, you will not be the same person you were before. You will learn the most from this person. They will show you who you are, who you aren't, and who you want to be. This person will help you identify and learn how to set hard boundaries. They will make you confront your flaws and insecurities and force you to take a good look at who you are and the life you have chosen to live.

The aftermath will force you to dissect all of your relationships. Hopefully these moments of reflection allow you to take accountability for your role in the chaos. You will be forced to identify the traits in each of you that caused the relationship to end. For that to happen you will have to spend some time by yourself. You must do the work. These failed relationships become mirrors. They highlight traits and patterns that need to be addressed. They expose parts of us that need healing.

The same is true for all your relationships, whether they involve business partners, family members, or friends. The people who hurt you deeply will test your limits, and even break you to the point where you think you won't be able to put yourself back together, but you will. You have no choice. People tend to think if a relationship does not last, it was a waste of time. You learn the most about people, including yourself, when there is conflict or things don't go according to plan. What may seem like a failed relationship, is nothing more than character development.

The key is to actually learn from these experiences. Apply what you've learned and make sure not to repeat the same mistakes again. When we refuse to learn the lesson, we will find ourselves meeting the same types of people, resulting in the same type of pain and hurt.

The only way to get past these difficult relationships is by going through them. Keep moving forward. Some life lessons cannot be learned without experiencing them yourself, and sometimes, living life means getting your heart and spirit broken into millions of pieces. Every interaction serves a purpose. Every relationship teaches you something about yourself. They force you to become intentional and practice discernment. They help you find the confidence to ask for exactly what you need and want from your friends, business partners, family members, and spouse. These interactions help identify what your boundaries need to be and how to set them. They help you become a better judge of character by recognizing red flags and acknowledging the green ones. Remember, insanity is doing the same things over and over while expecting different results. These lessons may not feel good in the moment, but they are essential lessons needed for real growth and accountability.

Failed relationships can also serve as a necessary wake-up call. They force us to make vital changes in the way we interact, and sometimes in the way we love. Some of us were not lucky enough to grow up with examples of healthy long-term relationships, so we had to learn through trial and error. We had to teach ourselves. Yes, we might hit a couple of roadblocks and encounter some shady characters along the way. Without these experiences, we will never develop the muscle memory or have the battle scars that serve as reminders of what we've lived through.

Chapter 10: Tired of Being Strong

We never realize how strong we are until strength is the only option we have left. Strength does not just show up overnight; it is built brick-by-brick over time. It is built steadily through life's curveballs and obstacles. You will be tested, and unfortunately, you aren't the one who decides what those tests will be. Life is the teacher, and sometimes we are the unwilling students.

On the bright side, the struggles you have endured over the years have become the foundation for the strength you embody today. We all have the capacity to be strong, but some of us have yet to discover our strength, but it is there, and it will surface in the exact moment it is needed. Some may be stronger than others, simply because their personal experiences have required them to be. Strength is that extra set of batteries that keeps us going when things get rough. It helps us to keep fighting the good fight. It's the little voice in our heads that screams, "Don't give up!" at the very moment we need to hear it.

Although strength is an integral part of our lives, it is also one of our most misunderstood character traits. Many of us measure strength by the amount of suffering we can endure, but is that really strength? They say you should fight for the things and people you want, but are "they" right? This thought process may be flawed. Sometimes we confuse fighting with begging or better yet, fear. The fear of letting go, the fear of missing out on an opportunity, or the fear of not being included. Are you fighting the good fight, or are you begging and forcing things you need to release? Are you scared to let go of that person, job, opportunity, idea, or project? Are you holding on so tight you are causing your own suffering? Are you being so "strong," you forget to be present, honest, and accountable?

We fear the unknown. People, things, jobs, and opportunities come and go. People will hurt you. People will walk out of your life without giving you any notice and without your permission. You will be disappointed. These are all part of this beautiful thing we call life. Although it may sting and seem unfair, we have to be thankful things do not always work out how we imagined or wanted them to. Sometimes what we want in the moment, what we are fighting so hard to keep in our lives, may not be meant for us or may be detrimental to our well-being.

There are people you must walk away from. You may miss them, crave their presence and energy, regardless of how they treat you. Nothing lasts forever. The good nor the bad. When you come to this realization, your world opens. When you realize anything and everything you force will not last, your need to control outcomes loosens. The desire to let things flow increases. Suffering for the sake of attachment becomes a thought of the past. After you have given something or someone your all, you need to recognize when there is no reason to fight any longer. No need to compromise.

You need to recognize when too many boundaries have been crossed. You need to recognize when too many promises have been broken. You need to recognize that sometimes what you are holding onto is no longer aligned with who you are or who you are becoming. When you reach that point, it is time to pick up what is left and walk away. But how do you know?

Although it is different for each person, when the memories of a person or thing are better than the reality of the actual person, it might be time to move on. So often, we hold on to how things used to be, we become blinded to the fact they have changed.

We get so lost in the past we are unable to see the reality of the present or the possibilities of the future. Instead of walking away and starting anew we continue to fight for the past, not realizing it's long gone. Walking away often takes more strength and courage than staying. Knowing when to throw in the towel is just as important, maybe more important, than knowing when to hold on for dear life. If you hold on for too long, you will continue to lose yourself. Holding on to a ghost or memory should never cost you your peace of mind, health, dignity, or integrity.

It is difficult to let go when you have invested time, energy, money, and hope in a business, job, or relationship. You don't want to start over or see your efforts go to waste. Every experience serves a purpose and nothing we do goes to waste, it's all a part of our journey. While it may seem self-sacrificing to hold on and fight, you must be clear about what you are fighting for. If that person or thing is harmful to your mental, emotional, financial, or spiritual well-being, it is time to reevaluate any further investment.

Just walk away they say. You know better. You deserve more. That sounds good, but it's easier said than done, especially when your heart, time, and emotions are involved. I remember not having the strength to walk away and blaming "love."

I remember making excuses for all the red flags I saw and felt, simply because I did not want to lose the person or time I'd invested. I remember ignoring the advice and concern of friends. I remember it all. I was in love, and no one could tell me any different.

Everyone goes through one relationship that literally takes them to hell and back, or at least right to its gates, before they wake up and realize they've been holding on to something and someone they should have let go of a long time ago. I used to think strength meant not giving up. But as I've gotten older, I have learned real strength is being able to recognize when something or someone is no longer serving you.

We cannot live the full lives we desire if we are too busy giving our time and energy to things that distract and drain. We cannot become who we are meant to be if we are so focused on who and what once was. My favorite distraction at one point in my life was a 5'11" handsome man with a beard who was a smooth talker and as manly as they came. He was my everything, at least I thought so. Things were complicated, and when I say complicated; I mean they were bad. This particular relationship resulted in years of unresolved trauma. It's funny how time, growth, and a good heartbreak wakes you up.

The fear of letting go wasn't just an issue in my personal life, it also affected my professional life. I remember being initially drawn in by the allure of working for a prestigious company with a great title. It did not take long before reality set in, and I found myself in a toxic and downright nasty work environment. I felt stuck, and undervalued. I wanted something new but was scared because this is what I had prayed for.

When things start falling apart, instead of stopping to ask why, we hold on for dear life to jobs, careers, and people that are not aligned with the people we are becoming. Change is hard but remaining in a situation that feels like a constant fight can have long-term implications for your career and your health.

The same is true in relationships. As painful as it is, you have to make the choice to walk away. This will be difficult, but there is no price too high for your peace of mind. There is no badge of honor for staying longer than you should!

There is strength in endings.

Chapter 11: Forgiveness is a Form of Healing

Better days are coming. You must choose to let go of pain, resentment, and disappointment. Let go of memories and people from your past. Do not allow life to fly past you because you are too focused on what once was. Get out of your own way. Are you stopping yourself from being happy and creating new memories because of your inability to let go and move on? Focusing on things that have already happened or no longer matter is a surefire way to self-sabotage and deter any possible progression or breakthrough. Why punish your present or future self for past mistakes? Your past is full of lessons and experiences that become tools to be utilized in the next phase of your life. Your past should never be used as an anchor that weighs you down or hinders you from accomplishing, experiencing, living, or loving.

Our experiences are meant to make us wiser and stronger; they are not meant to be an excuse or crutch. When we become prisoners of our past, we not only repeat the very suffering we wish to escape, but we also invite future suffering. Yes, you should reflect on your past. Yes, you have the right to acknowledge past pain and hurt. But to what extent? Feel your emotions, live, and walk in your truth, but never allow your emotions or past experiences to cripple you from living a bigger, better, more fulfilling life. Do not allow past scars to stop you before you even get started.

The past can keep us ashamed, isolated, and afraid. Do whatever it takes to heal, do whatever it takes to come to terms with the reality that is your life. Get closure, in whatever ways are meaningful and accessible. Take the time you need to process your emotions, even if that means self-pity for a few days, weeks, or months. But sooner or later you need to shed that last tear, send that last text, or end that toxic friendship.

Stop replaying what ifs that never were. Feel the emotions, learn the lessons, but then put yourself back together. Get back to a place where you feel whole, get back to a place where you are in control of your emotions. Do not allow the moments, days, weeks, or months of pain to keep you from experiencing the joy and happiness that is on the other side of healing, ownership, and real accountability. Remember, there is power in owning your mistakes; there is power in taking control. No experience is wasted, it all serves a purpose.

It's so easy to focus on all the things that have happened to us instead of realizing everything is happening for and because of us. The good, the bad, the questionable. If we played a sizzle reel of each of our lives, not only would it show all the things people have said and done to us, but it would also highlight all we've have said and done, including things we may now regret. Some find it difficult to move on due to guilt. That guilt can be especially daunting when you are being constantly reminded about what you did or the hurt you felt, and even caused.

The question then becomes, when are you free to move on? When should you no longer engage in conversations about the past hurt and pain you've caused? Of course, this differs on a case-by-case basis but if we had to create a general rule, here it is. If there is honest and respectful dialogue, revisiting the past can be beneficial when it can help resolve issues and foster healing. Sometimes healing means parting ways with unanswered questions.

Remember closure takes on many forms, and the result may not always be what you imagined. When the past is being turned into a weapon or crutch it might be time to move on. It might be time to forgive yourself and let it go. Constantly revisiting something, with no solution or healing in sight will do more harm than good. When you allow people to hold things over your head or play puppet master with your emotions, you unintentionally give them power to use whenever and however they please. In the wrong hands, this can lead to emotional manipulation.

When it comes to hurt you have caused, your obligation is to acknowledge your words or actions, and genuinely make amends to the best of your ability. That's what accountability is all about—taking ownership, actively seeking solutions, and moving on. If you have done that, you are free. You are not required to constantly reopen old wounds and be held prisoner by those who refuse to let the past go.

Why do we hold on to the past? The answer is familiarity and lack of accountability. We know the ins and outs of what already happened, who was involved, and even the outcome. The past is safer because it doesn't change, you are reliving the same story over and over. There are no surprises. When you allow yourself to be stuck in this time warp, you release yourself from the responsibility that comes with living in the present and facing reality.

Living in the present requires you to come face to face with the facts of your life and make active decisions. When you are focused on today and looking out toward the future, you have no choice but to deal with the past to some degree and create a plan to move forward. Let go of yesterday and take the reins of your life. Yes, there is risk and fear that comes with the unknown, but so what? Deciding to let go is refusing to be a victim. It's deciding to purposely take on the risk of possible new hurt, disappointment, or pain. We fear what we do not know and what we do not understand. Our pasts are familiar; they are our comfort zones. The future is filled with so many unknowns, and sometimes sticking with the devil you know feels like the safe bet.

The truth is, life is going to continue to happen whether you participate or not. You must allow yourself the space and opportunity to truly create the life you want, and sometimes that requires deserting our past selves. You can't move forward if you are constantly looking back. The best thing we can do is accept, embrace, control what we can, get prepared, and release everything else. Get ready to experience the newness that comes from letting go and starting over.

Break free of the hurt. Break free of the pain. Forgive those who have brought tears to your eyes and forget them if necessary. Let go and let God. Not for them, but for yourself. Not because they deserve your forgiveness, but because you deserve happiness and peace. You deserve to heal.

Forgive yourself. You deserve to wake up every morning without hatred in your heart or regret on your mind. You deserve to wake up knowing you have done everything in your power to attain joy and happiness.

We are not our mistakes. Show yourself grace.

Over the years, I have had to repeatedly remind myself to let the past go. Letting go is a process. It takes time to convince yourself certain experiences are best left forgiven or forgotten. It's something you learn to do not because you want to do it, but because you must. Like most of you, I've had my share of betrayal from friends and family, business partners, mentors, etc. Some experiences sting more than others, some I'll never forget about.

The summer right before high school, I was sexually assaulted by someone I thought was a friend. You would think that would be the most traumatizing part of the story, but it wasn't the molestation I had difficulty coming to terms with or releasing. It was the circumstances leading up to it. I was put in a compromising and dangerous situation by someone I considered a sister, a close friend, a best friend. Someone whose family treated me like family. We were as thick as thieves, but none of this mattered. Unfortunately, I learned my well-being would always be an afterthought when it came to her personal desires.

My best friend at the time put me in a situation that changed my life and was the catalyst for the trust issues I still deal with to this day. She put her own feelings, enjoyment, and sexual promiscuity before my safety. That day forever changed my perception of women and began my distrust and disgust for men. I thought these feelings would last forever, rightfully so.

One day, after years of anger and therapy, it hit me, I had to let it go. I let go of the guilt and shame I had for allowing myself to be put in such a dangerous situation. I let go of my hatred towards those two individuals because it was stopping me from creating and maintaining healthy, meaningful relationships. Although I will always remember what happened, I had to let go of how I allowed it to control my life. I had to relearn how to love, how to trust, and how to feel safe.

To get my life back, I had to let go.

Chapter 12: Pride Hurts and Pride Saves

Pride. The double-edged sword. It can either stop you from making some of the worst decisions of your life, or it can make you miss out on life-changing opportunities. Having too much pride might cost you your happiness, while having too little can make you susceptible to being constantly taken advantage of. The key is balance.

When was the last time you wanted to call someone, or ask for help? But because of your pride, you refused to pick up the phone or send that email? Instead of reaching out you listened to that little voice in your head that speaks to your ego instead of relying on your logic or heart to guide you. What voice? You know, the one that tells you things like No, they should call you, you do not want to seem desperate. You are too good, you can do it on your own, you're going to look weak if you reach out. That is the voice we have all heard at least once, some more frequently than others.

Some of us listen to this voice, not realizing it is the same voice that is stopping us from growing and living full lives. It is the voice holding us back from going to the next level in our careers or from mending an important relationship. We often forget true love and care does not involve pride, but, instead, requires vulnerability. If you allow this voice to guide your actions, any chance at genuine love or professional growth will be destroyed prematurely by misdirected pride.

Excessive pride, if not tamed, can look like selfishness. When we are too prideful, we become so consumed with our own wants and needs we forget about others, including the very people we love the most. We become cold and dismissive towards the needs of other people. Our pride can have us so focused on not looking needy that we allow life-changing opportunities slip through our fingers.

Pride is dangerous, especially in love and business. We must always be aware of how we allow pride and ego to affect our personal and professional relationships. Achieving your end goal should always be more important than preserving your pride. We must be mindful not to allow our ego to drive our life's decisions — especially those that could have long-term consequences.

Although pride can be cancerous, it should not be completely discarded. Instead, it must be managed and controlled. There is a time and place for us to lean into our pride.

If you are like most people, keeping your pride in check is a constant job. On one hand it can be detrimental to our growth, on the other hand it may stop us from doing stupid things we may later regret.

It's important to take pride in the things you accomplish or the projects you create, but you should never allow pride to be the motive behind important life decisions. Pride can save you just as quickly as it can destroy you. Know when to bring it to the party we call life and know when to leave it at the door like an uninvited guest. Keep it under wraps! Like anything else, too much can be dangerous. Is your pride stopping you from making the necessary decisions to improve your life? Is your pride stopping you from reaching your fullest potential? Is pride blocking your blessing? Take a second to think about it. Are you running away from things and people because you are too stubborn to acknowledge your prideful behavior?

Pride is such a layered virtue and personality trait because it often serves as a window into a person's past. We are human and have all made mistakes. Most of us have had traumatizing experiences that have left us feeling distrustful and guarded. This can lead people to build walls of protection that manifest in the form of pride. Some of us have felt so much hurt in the past we refuse to feel that pain again, so we use pride as a defense mechanism. It becomes an excuse not to let people get too close or influence our emotions. Pride is such an intricate emotion.

We are all multifaceted beings. The most prideful person you know may also be the person with the most insecurity or the one who has experienced the most betrayal. We are all going through something behind closed doors where others can't see, and because of that, we respond to life experiences in different ways.

I am sure you have had at least one experience that felt devastating. Perhaps you have tried to take a leap of faith and it backfired. Things may have gone so poorly it forced you to hide in shame. Rather than seeking comfort from friends and family, you hid behind pride and ego. You pushed people away without uttering a word. You became so guarded, no one would even attempt to approach. This is where your pride does more harm than good. Especially when it is rooted in fear.

Instead of saying, "I am scared, I am embarrassed, I am hurt," we hide behind pride and ego. I have been guilty of this myself. There was a time when I was so afraid of trying new things and meeting new people I would have anxiety attacks and completely shut down. I masked my fear with very mean-spirited jokes about others or self-deprecating comments about myself. I would belittle those around me instead of opening up to them. When this happened, my pride would be right on my heels and spring into action to put up a facade to justify my actions.

This often resulted in people labeling me as stuck up, rude, mean, or a know-it-all. All of these labels were the farthest from my truth. I was just a little girl trapped in an adult's body who was too afraid to be myself. Having too much pride can transform your naturally loving and open heart into a shielded and cynical one. Do not miss the blessings God has tailor-made for you. Do not allow fear to control your life. Do not let pride win.

I remember when Hurricane Sandy hit the East Coast. Officials advised everyone in areas of NJ and NY to get to safety or leave the area if possible. Like the prideful idiot I was at the time, I did not leave, even though I was in the path of the storm. I refused to leave my apartment. Unfortunately, my neighborhood was impacted by the hurricane, and I was without power and access to food for almost two weeks. At the time, I had family in Maryland who told me I could stay with them until things got back to normal, but I refused. I did not want to be a burden, and I did not want to ask for help.

Thinking back, I was being ridiculous and filled with pride. I did not want to burden others. For some reason, a lot of people see me as a strong and independent woman, and although I am, I sometimes find myself in situations where I am afraid and unable to ask for help because I fear disappointing people or worse, embarrassing myself. I did not want to appear weak or seem reliant on others. I didn't want to appear needy and admit I had made the wrong decision.

My pride stopped me from being safe. As a result, I was without heat, food, or shelter simply because I did not want to admit I was in need. I allowed my pride to take over my common sense. Even amid a natural disaster, I was more concerned about how the optics looked to family and friends rather than making sure I was safe. How often do we suffer just to keep up appearances instead of being open and honest? We subconsciously allow our pride to control decisions that can impact the trajectory of our lives.

Chapter 13: Feeding Your Fears

Fear is a beast. Everyone fears getting hurt, everyone fears failing. Everyone fears disappointing the people we care about. No one wants to constantly open up and be vulnerable to people or become their emotional punching bag. We are afraid of letting people in. When we give fear control over our lives, we are no longer in the driver's seat. Surrendering control to fear is just as dangerous as allowing pride to make decisions for us. When we succumb to fear we give up our power, and our voice.

Fear is a silent killer. It can cripple the wealthiest and the strongest. Fear can steal every moment of joy. It stops people from speaking up. Fear prolongs suffering. Fear will stop you before you even truly get started. Fear will have you looking back at the years wasted and the opportunities missed. Do not allow fear to stop you from doing what you want to do. Even more importantly, don't allow your fear to stop you from doing what you need to do. Fear can lead you down a rabbit hole of unknowns. It can paralyze you.

Fear has power because we give it power. We allow the seed of fear to be planted, then we water it and feed it, granting it space to take on a life of its own. Fear becomes so dominating it no longer asks for our permission to show up. It just exists. Fear can grow from the smallest whisper and the slightest insecurities. Without us taking notice, it becomes a disease spreading to every aspect of our life. It can be so crippling we no longer seek solutions; we just want an escape.

When fear is allowed to lead, you surrender your free will. Your life is no longer yours to live; instead, you start making decisions that drive you further away from the people and things you care about. This can look like staying in spaces that no longer serve you or not living up to your full potential. You've heard it before; growth happens outside of your comfort zone. It's great when we feel secure and comfortable, but this can also delay our breakthrough. How can you find out what you are capable of if you do not try? Allowing fear to control what you do puts you at risk for allowing life to happen to you instead of for you.

You must fight fear consistently, and intentionally. Fighting fear is an internal battle. You are the only one who can overcome your fear, you are the only one who can stop your fears from taking over your life. To fight fear, we must first acknowledge it exists. The process is simple, but not easy. Fear, like pride, can serve a purpose. It is not about getting rid of our fears. Instead, it's about reminding yourself that fear has no power over your life. Fear is not a decision maker. Confront your fear, speak to it, then destroy it. Most times, our fears are rooted in things that have not happened and because of this, we must recognize fear is self-inflicted and based on feelings and not facts. Fear is a tactic used to cripple and delay. If you hand over your life to fear, you will become so afraid of even trying you will do nothing.

Fear holds you hostage. Most of us fear things because we fear failure. Sorry to burst your bubble, but you are going to fail many times in your lifetime. It is part of the process. Failure is not a reason to give up. You owe it to yourself to keep trying. It is much better to live life saying, "Wow I can't believe I did that!" rather than living a life filled with "what ifs." What if I took that job? What if I went on that trip? What if I loved more? What if I had tried a little harder? That is no way to go through life, because you will never have an answer. You will be left with nothing but regret because you let life pass you by. You must give yourself a chance. At least try.

Are you living? Are you having a full human experience or are you just existing?

Faith and fear both require believing in things that may not have happened yet, but one provides the ammo to keep going while the other gives you every reason to stop. The beauty is each time you confront fear, you get better at recognizing its tricks, and instead of it becoming a full-on stop sign for you, it turns into a reminder to focus on past and future wins, and not the potential doom you have dreamt up. Keep going. Regardless of how scared you become. You must push past the fear. You must live your life.

One of the key differences between those who are happy and successful and those who aren't is how they respond to fear. Some people allow their fears to control them, while others see their fears as a challenge and become determined to conquer them. Will your fear stop you or motivate you? The choice is yours.

As silly as it sounds, I once feared falling in love. I feared falling for someone so deeply because I worried it would come to an end. I come from a huge family, which typically means stepparents, stepsiblings, and torn relationships. Although my parents loved me and did whatever was in their power to make sure I was happy growing up, things were not always sunshine and rainbows.

When my mother and I moved to this country, everything was new, everything was strange. At first things were tricky, but we adjusted. Then my parents got a divorce, which led to blended families. Our family dynamic took a turn for the worse when my father passed away. His passing caused ripple effects of grief throughout our family. My brothers and I lost our father, my mother lost her first love, and my aunties/uncles lost their brother.

That was my first experience losing someone who mattered to me, and it was the one person who mattered the most to me. When he died, everything changed. The once semi-happily blended family was now overcome with chaos and unanswered questions. My father was the person who held us together, and when he passed, we also lost the glue that kept us intact. From that moment on there was an emotional wall built up around me, I let no one in. It became extremely difficult to connect with other humans, especially men. I never allowed myself to open up to others because I feared the day they would leave, either by choice or by premature death. That fear stayed with me and is still something I deal with today. When that fear became so intense it stopped me from experiencing true joy and intimacy, I knew I needed help. Something had to give.

Chapter 14: Vision Is a Must

We all need vision, whether it's a vision for how we want to be treated, how we want our lives to look/feel or how we want to impact the world. If you don't have one, create one. When looking for that perfect spouse, friend, or business partner, there are certain things that should be standard. Their vision for themselves should be one of the key factors in determining what role they should play in your life. The quality of the people you surround yourself with plays a vital role in who you become. Do they have a vision? Some people are not on a mission, some don't have anything to believe in or fight for. Some people are just going through the motions and doing just what it takes to make it to the next day. Although that is not a bad thing, it can be a hinderance to those of us who are purpose or vision led. When people have nothing to believe in or strive for, they tend to move through life a little differently. There is less intention behind their decisions. They have chosen to live with less care than the rest of us.

Having a clear vision for your life helps center you as a person. Vision along with purpose makes dealing with the ups and downs that come with life a little more tolerable. When you know you are living for something more than just a bi-weekly paycheck, likes on Instagram, a relationship, or your current circumstances, you are not easily swayed by the emotions or situations that may otherwise deter you from your path and goals. When purpose drives a person, they are no longer living by the same set of rules as those around them. Their code of conduct changes, their motivation changes, their actions change.

Some of us are driven by the need to be accepted, others seek financial stability or the desire of having a family of our own. Not everyone has the same motivation, and because of this, you never know what a person is willing to do, say, or risk to get where they want to go. Although you do not have to agree with everything the people in your life do, it's important to know why they do certain things or at least understand the type of people they are. Knowing their vision or their motivations will help you evaluate what position they should or are even capable of playing in your life. Everyone does not deserve the same level of access to you, especially on this healing, and accountability journey. It's on you to determine who should stay or go.

Your vision is what you are passionate about, what drives you, what encourages you, it dominates your thoughts and gives you energy to keep going when things get tough. Over the years, I've realized people with vision often desire to create things that not only benefit them, but others as well. It is always a joy to witness people who have made a conscious decision to lend their talent, skill, and ideas to positively impact others. That selflessness has the ability to influence the lives of many. That is what having vision and living a purpose-driven life is all about. Not everyone can submit to their vison, it is easy to become distracted or to be led astray. It's easier to live without a care or concern for others.

We live in a society where individuality has been replaced with selfishness. Many people lack common decency and consideration for one another. Some of us are so blinded by the need for instant gratification and individual praise, we become unable and unwilling to see the bigger picture. The journey may not be linear, and life may not always go as planned, but clarity allows you to keep moving forward, despite the curve balls thrown your way. Having vision gives you a sense of purpose. That purpose is the reason you can still smile in the midst of chaos.

No one wants to continue running in endless circles with nothing to be achieved or show for our efforts. Believe in yourself; create the life you desire, do not settle for the one given to you. We cannot allow moments of uncertainty to cloud our judgment and blur our vision.

Having a vison and actively pursuing it can be a difficult task for many. People may plant seeds of doubt that make you question yourself or tempt you to give up. Dreaming is the easy part. The hard part is consistently showing up, doing the work, and staying focused on the vision even when things look shaky. The real work is believing in yourself when no one else does. Execute the vison, it's not enough to dream.

You must make the plan and stay the course. Do what you said you would do. Hold yourself accountable. When you are doing something just for the sake of doing it, you tend to approach it callously, with no real concern because you may not care about the outcome. When you are doing something connected to your purpose that ignites you to the core, you become invested, you care. You care because you know the impact it can have on not just yourself but the world. You care because you understand there is a bigger picture. There is something more at stake—the vision.

I remember when I was around fifteen, and I thought I knew exactly how my life would turn out. I knew I would go to college in New York, meet someone, graduate, make a lot of money, and I would be set for life. Next would come marriage with the love of my life, my first love. In my fairy tale, we would have children, stable jobs, travel, and live happily ever after.

When we are young and are painting the pictures of what we think our ideal life is going to look like, we forget the most important thing: life is unpredictable. Not only is life unpredictable, but change is the only constant. Regardless of what is going on in our lives, we can always count on things to constantly change. The people around you change, your wants and needs change, you change. Because of this, our desires may change along the way. The lives we wanted when we were fifteen years old change by the time we are twenty-five, and again by the time we are thirty-five. Yes, at the time I loved that job and person, but do I think the person I am today, and that version of my life would have worked? Hell no. At the core of my childish hopes for my future was the longing to be happy, successful, and loved. So, although the details of what that looked like may have changed, the vison did not. I am glad things did not work out exactly as I hoped. I thank God for who I am today. The vision and the purpose attached to my life now is so much clearer. I am creating a life that forces people to believe in good people again, that forces people to believe in God.

Chapter 15: The Power of Patience

Patience is a virtue many of us never learned. Patience is the ability to wait graciously. Patience is knowing everything happens when and how it is meant to. It's the ability to wait without anger, frantic behavior, or allowing your thoughts to get the best of you. Having real patience takes time to develop. Patience is normally something we develop through life experiences and time. Really, that is all patience is. It's time.

Time is in control of it all. It controls everything. You cannot buy it, you cannot slow it down, and you cannot make it go any faster. Time is independent of everything and everyone. No one can control time; you're going to have to wait on time whether you want to or not. The one thing you do have control over is what you do while you wait. You can choose to use your time wisely or not, but time slows down for no one.

Although I have slowly learned the value of patience, it is something I constantly struggle with and must be mindful of daily. Simple things like waiting for a phone call or email to be returned can easily lead to negative thoughts, and misplaced feelings.

Learning to have patience with people, and more importantly myself, has been a reoccurring theme in my life.

Imagine being a perfectionist who lacks patience. It's probably one of the worst possible personality trait combinations a person could have. Needing to see things happen quickly and perfectly, does nothing but cause unnecessary frustration and chaos. My lack of patience has made so many of my life experiences incredibly tougher than they needed to be. My lack of patience has stopped me from enjoying some of my most special moments, because I was constantly thinking about what was next instead of what was happening right before my eyes.

Once you develop patience, even just a smidge, it gives you a whole new perspective on life. You come to realize things happen whether you are ready for them to or not. Life moves on with or without you. Life happens when it's going to happen, and how it's going to happen. All you can do is prepare to the best of your ability and enjoy each moment as much as possible. Patience is the ability to respect time and all its power.

Each one of us is given the same twenty-four hours. The same 1,400 minutes. The same 86,400 seconds. Regardless of how intelligent, strong, attractive, or wealthy you are, time is in control, and we are at its mercy. No man or woman walking this earth has the power to control or thoroughly understand time. The only way to increase your patience is to constantly put yourself in situations that require you to wait. Time answers to no one.

If I didn't know what patience was before, I am well acquainted with her now. I say her because it's been said that wisdom is a woman, so I just know her sister must be patience. During the process of writing this book, from development, editing, and finally publishing, I've experienced almost every emotion. From confused, distraught, stressed, happiness, excited, disappointed, broke (ha, is broke an emotion? lol), I have literally felt it all. This book has been in the works for at least four years now and has seen many versions and edits. I was in my own way, because I am an avid overthinker. I had to get to a point where I was happy and content with what I had done, otherwise, another four years would pass. If I kept this book unfinished and under wraps any longer, it might never have seen the light of day. I would have gone down another rabbit hole of thoughts, emotions, and edits. Realizing everything happens when and how it is meant to is something I had to come to terms with, especially as it relates to time. Regardless of what we do, we will always be at the mercy of the clock. There have been times when I have literally stopped and ripped out pages of books, trashed whole journals, yelled in empty rooms because I was unable to sit still. My thoughts were eating me alive which caused deep anxiety. Patience often felt like one of those things God decided not to give me, until I learned I was fighting a losing battle. I had to learn to literally submit to time. The only solution is to let go and let God. Patience is not the ability to wait, because you have no choice but to wait. Patience is what you choose to do while you wait.

Chapter 16: No, It's Me

We are a combination of experiences and decisions. Your life is your life, and until you come to terms with that, you will constantly seek approval from those who may or may not understand or even care. We all have something in common—pain and choices.

Each of us has been through a rough patch. We have all felt the wrath of life and have been hit with a few curve balls. We have had days when we felt overwhelmed or alone. We have had something, or someone taken from us. Whether it is your favorite toy as a child or your favorite person as an adult. Pain may be one of the very few universal truths we can all relate to, regardless of your race, gender, religion, economic status, etc. Our pain connects us, and makes us human!

It's you. You have the power. You are the power. You are in control.

This is your life, take control. As redundant as this may seem, it is something that needs to be said over and over until it is embedded in your mind. This is your life. YOUR LIFE. Not your mother's, father's, brother's, sister's, teacher's, coach's, wife's, or husband's, not even your children's. This is your life, and you will be held accountable for every decision you make and don't make. How that accountability unfolds is up to you, you can lean in or fight it, but for every action there is a consequence, good or bad. Accountability is accepting responsibility, even if you are not at fault. The good news is that this is your life. You don't have to wait for anyone else to decide or save you. At any moment, with one decision, you can regain control.

You are the answer to your problems. That's what life comes down to—owning our own crap. Owning your flaws and imperfections, and still loving who you are. It's so easy to point the finger at others. As willing as we are to take the applause when things are going great, we also have to be just as willing to take the necessary hits when they are not. When you are able to accept the role you play in your life, things begin to happen; you begin changing. You must change. Life always demands change. When we can hold ourselves accountable for our mistakes and decisions, we take our power back. That is what this book is about, acknowledging your power, and taking it back.

No one has it all figured out. We are all just trying to find our place in this thing we call life. This book isn't meant to condemn you. It's meant to be the beginning of a new chapter in your life, the chapter that requires you to take a good and hard look at the woman or man you are and really ask yourself the tough questions—the questions you fear hearing the answers to. Once you do that, you become unstoppable. If you want that type of power, it starts with having these difficult conversations, being honest and then holding yourself accountable. Thank you for going on this journey with me, but more importantly, thank you for going on the journey with yourself.

ABOUT THE AUTHOR

Ann Akinnuoye is a first-generation Nigerian daughter and one of eight children in a uniquely blended family. She moved to the United States at the age of four. At the age of nine, she lost her father who served as her safe place. This unexpected loss set the foundation for her relationship with God, her deep desire to understand people, and her view of the world around her.

From a young age she has always had a direct and bold personality—a blessing and, sometimes, a curse both personally and professionally. Her journey to becoming a multifaceted marketing executive, investor, creative, and author has never been linear. From her start in finance to creating and leading award-winning campaigns and initiatives for some of the world's biggest Fortune 500 companies, she has had to constantly and intentionally pivot throughout uncharted waters.

Ann Akinnuoye has a desire to understand the "WHY" behind people and brands. This has allowed her to wear many hats across organizations that require not just strategy but exceptional execution. A big part of her personal and professional brand has been built around her ability to deliver with excellence, be accountable and consistent. Her point of view may not always be easy to hear, but it's always rooted in ensuring the people and organizations she works with are setting themselves up to not only deliver but to deliver with integrity. She adamantly believes good business always starts with good people; you cannot separate the two.

Through many varied life experiences, Ann has realized, at the core, we all need and desire love. She understands the power we each have, and how frequently that power is so easily given away due to the lack of accountability. Ann has been on a never-ending journey of living in her truth while also learning to give people the same grace God continues to give her.

Acknowledgements

I would like to begin by expressing my gratitude to God for consistently sustaining and protecting me throughout the various phases of life. Without my relationship with God, I would not be here today.

I am forever indebted to my family, who have always supported me and been my constant anchor through all circumstances. My friends, who have made a point to celebrate me, even when I did not want to celebrate myself, you have all been a part of this journey.

I thank you all for loving and encouraging me. Thank you for simply allowing me to be myself.

Lastly, to the readers who took the time out of their lives to join me on this literary adventure, I am forever grateful.

To stay connected with Ann please visit: Akinconsults.com.

If this book has been helpful to you, please consider leaving a review on the site where you purchased it. It only takes a minute. But reviews are the most effective way to share this book with others.

www.ingramcontent.com/pod-product-compliance
Lightning Source LLC
Chambersburg PA
CBHW071348150726
47997CB00002B/896